Environmental Justice Program Comprehensive Management Study

I0425901

Final Report

Prepared for:
U.S. Environmental Protection Agency
Office of Environmental Justice
Washington, DC

Prepared by:
Timothy Fields, Jr.
Tetra Tech EM Inc.
Reston, VA

Submitted on:
May 26, 2004

Table of Contents

    Appendix 1: List and Schedule of EPA Deputy Assistant Administrator (DAA) and Deputy Regional Administrator (DRA) Discussions

    Appendix 2: Areas of Inquiry for EPA Deputy Assistant Administrator (DAA) and Deputy Regional Administrator (DRA) Discussions

    Appendix 3: Template for Summary of EPA Deputy Assistant Administrator (DAA) and Deputy Regional Administrator (DRA) Discussions

    Appendix 4: List of EPA Headquarters Program and Regional Office FY 2004-2005 EJ Action Plans and FY 2003 EJ Progress Reports Reviewed for the Management Study

    Appendix 5: List of Follow-up Data Requested from EPA Headquarters Program and Regional Office EJ Coordinators

    Appendix 6: Various Tables and Charts Summarizing Data and Other Information Gathered and Reviewed As Part of the Management Study

Environmental Justice Program Comprehensive Management Study

Final Report

Section 1: Background, Approach and Report Organization

This section provides background on the Environmental Justice (EJ) Program Comprehensive Management Study, the method by which the management study was undertaken, and how the management study report is organized. The goal of the management study is to identify areas of improvement in EPA environmental justice program integration, and to provide associated recommendations to the U.S. Environmental Protection Agency (EPA).

1.1 MANAGEMENT STUDY BACKGROUND

This section describes the recent events leading to EPA's necessity to undertake this management study.

In light of the recent EPA Inspector General's (IG) report on environmental justice, *EPA Needs to Consistently Implement the Intent of the Executive Order on Environmental Justice*, Report No. 2004-P-00007, March 1, 2004, the Agency, through the Office of Environmental Justice (OEJ), agreed to conduct a management study of Headquarters program and Regional office funding, staffing and organization of environmental justice.

The IG stated in their report that "Environmental Justice is not staffed, funded or organized as an Agency priority. In such case, the Agency is hampered in its ability to implement the EJ Action Plans." In particular, the IG noted the following weaknesses:

- Staffing at the Headquarters program and Regional office levels are not under the control of OEJ; rather, they are dependent upon the Assistant Administrator (AA) or Regional Administrator (RA).

- EJ action plans show staffing disparities in Full Time Equivalents (FTE) in each Regional office.

- Within the EPA Regions, funding for EJ positions are obtained from their discretionary funds.[1]

- Within the EPA Headquarters offices, funding for EJ activities are obtained from their individual program accounts.

- OEJ does not provide funding and has no authority over the Headquarters programs and Regional offices regarding efforts to integrate EJ.

- The Environmental Justice Executive Steering Committee makes environmental decisions on a consensus basis.

As part of EPA's response to the IG report, the Agency, through OEJ, agreed to conduct a management study and gather information on the organizational infrastructure, staffing and funding levels, and methods of accountability of each Headquarters program and Regional office. Specifically, EPA agreed this management study would examine the following:

- Headquarters program and Regional office funding and staffing for EJ activities to ensure that adequate resources are available to fully implement the Agency's EJ program

- Benefits of designating qualified and committed full time employees (FTEs) to manage the EJ program in each Headquarters program and Regional office

- Opportunities to integrate EJ into the strategic and operating plan processes

- Needs for and benefits of shifting resources and formal reporting structures to improve the integration of EJ into core programs in the Headquarters programs and Regional offices

This information will help the Agency identify areas of improvement in its overall EJ program. The remainder of this report delves into ascertaining the ability of each Headquarters program and Regional office to effectively integrate EJ into its policies, programs and activities, and provides recommendations for moving closer to that overarching Agency goal.

---

[1] Regional offices noted during the management study that this is an incorrect statement in the IG report. Funding comes from redirection of FTEs from other program areas.

1.2 MANAGEMENT STUDY APPROACH

This section describes the approach applied to conduct the Environmental Justice Program Comprehensive Management Study. Appendix 1 provides the areas of inquiry for discussions with each EPA Deputy Assistant Administrator (DAA) and Deputy Regional Administrator (DRA), as well as other crucial information collected from EPA Headquarters and Regional Environmental Justice Coordinators.

The study was organized and led by Mr. Timothy Fields, Jr. of Tetra Tech EM Inc. (Tetra Tech), and formerly the EPA Assistant Administrator for the Office of Solid Waste and Emergency Response (OSWER). A small team of Tetra Tech staff supported Mr. Fields.

The study team had a limited timeframe for undertaking the management study. Mindful of this, the study team conducted a simplified, straightforward analysis to determine any trends, commonalities and differences of approach among Headquarters programs and Regional offices for the four primary areas of inquiry regarding their EJ program activities and requirements. Those areas included (1) organizational function and alignment; (2) staffing assignments and responsibilities; (3) resource planning and allocation; and (4) program integration and strategic direction.

The study team gathered information for this report using the following methods of inquiry:

1.2.1 One-on-One Discussions with EPA DAAs and DRAs

The study team conducted one-on-one discussions with each EPA DAA and DRA on organizational function and alignment, staffing assignments and responsibilities, resource planning and allocation, and program integration and strategic direction regarding their EJ program activities and requirements. Appendix 2 provides the list and schedule of discussions with EPA DAAs and DRAs. Each discussion with the EPA DAA or DRA lasted approximately 1 to 1½ hours, and most were performed by conference call. Instructions were given that each discussion should occur only with the DAA or DRA, in order that a frank and open discussion could occur and focus more exclusively on his or her experiences and understanding regarding the EJ program activities and requirements under his or her responsibility. Appendix 1 provides the specific lines of inquiry used during these discussions. The results of each discussion were recorded by a note-taker and compiled in a standard format, along the lines of inquiry identified above. Appendix 3 provides the sample template used for compiling the information gathered during each discussion.

1.2.2 In-depth Review of EPA Headquarters Program and Regional Office Fiscal Year (FY) 2004-2005 EJ Action Plans and FY 2003 Progress Reports

The study team performed an in-depth review of EPA Headquarters program and Regional office FY 2004-2005 EJ Action Plans and FY 2003 EJ Progress Reports. The study team was especially interested in obtaining information contained in the plans and progress reports regarding organizational and management approach and resources (people and dollars) allocated for EJ program activities and requirements. Pertinent information was compiled in tabular format, which is presented throughout the remainder of the report. This review was valuable and insightful, when supplemented with the EPA DAA and DRA discussions, in what level of understanding and engagement he or she had with guiding and influencing the preparation of the action plans and progress reports from an overall strategic standpoint. Appendix 4 provides the list of EJ action plans and progress reports reviewed.

1.2.3 Follow-up Data Requests to EPA Headquarters Program and Regional Office EJ Coordinators

The study team also performed a follow-up data request to EPA Headquarters program and Regional office EJ Coordinators for information that was either (1) not available during the one-on-one discussions with EPA DAAs and DRAs or (2) not readily available or included in the EPA Headquarters program and Regional office FY 2004-2005 EJ Action Plans and FY 2003 EJ Progress Reports. The study team was especially interested in obtaining more detailed and accurate information on FTEs actually devoted to EJ and to what extent formal position descriptions and performance evaluation factors actually took his or her EJ functions into consideration and account. Another important reason for this follow-up inquiry was to establish and document a clear and complete understanding of the actual resources (contract and grant dollars and other applicable resources) dedicated in each organization for EJ support. Appendix 5 provides the specific data requested from the EJ Coordinators.

1.2.4 Discussions on the EJ Program and OIG Report at the 2004 National Environmental Justice Advisory Council (NEJAC) Meeting in New Orleans, LA

Mr. Fields participated in two two-hour discussions on the EJ program and the OIG report at the National Environmental Justice Advisory Council (NEJAC) meeting in New Orleans, LA on April 12–16, 2004. These discussions were included in the agenda of the NEJAC meeting, and the results will be reflected in the meeting minutes prepared for the NEJAC meeting. Any additional insights gathered during these discussions and valuable to the findings and recommendations of this report are reflected herein.

1.2.5 Input Provided During the April 29, 2004 Meeting of the EPA Environmental Justice Executive Steering Committee in Washington, DC

The members of the Environmental Justice Executive Steering Committee present at the April 29, 2004 meeting provided additional insights and recommendations pertinent to this management study. These additional insights and recommendations were provided as part of a facilitated discussion regarding the OIG report, the Agency's response to the report, and this EJ Program Comprehensive Management Study. These additional insights and recommendations are also reflected herein.

1.3 MANAGEMENT STUDY REPORT ORGANIZATION

This management study report includes the following six sections:

Section 1 – Background, Approach and Report Organization

Section 2 – Designating Qualified and Committed Full Time Employees

Section 3 – Integrating EJ into Strategic and Operating Plans

Section 4 – Funding and Staffing for EJ

Section 5 – Shifting Resources and Formal Reporting Structures

Section 6 – Findings & Recommendations

Several Appendices also are included, providing further information gathered and analyzed during conduct of the management study, as well as the pertinent documents provided to and reviewed by the study team and that were crucial in preparing this management study report. The specific appendices are listed at the end of this report.

Section 2: Designating Qualified and Committed Full Time Employees

This section explores the area of designating qualified and committed full time employees (FTEs) to manage the EJ program in each Headquarters program and Regional office. The following provides a summary of the observations of the DAAs and DRAs, as well as pertinent data collected and assessed for this management study.

Consistency in the Designation and Allocation of FTEs for EJ Programs: Data collected for the management study, along with discussions with DAAs and DRAs, shows inconsistency in how FTEs for EJ programs are designated and allocated by Headquarters programs and Regional offices. There also is discrepancy in which FTEs are viewed as "core" to the implementation of EJ programs, versus which EJ FTEs are viewed as being a "collateral" part of the overall implementation of EPA programs. Some DAAs and DRAs noted that it could be a significant challenge to properly and consistently account for actual FTE expenditures for EJ programs, as well as assess whether those expenditures are adequate to accomplish EJ program functions and activities. There also are wide variations between Headquarters programs and Regional offices on the total number of FTEs devoted to EJ (see Section 4), including the EJ Coordinator and EJ support staff.

Responsibility for the Designation and Allocation of FTEs for EJ Programs: Nearly all DAAs and DRAs did not favor OEJ having complete responsibility or authority over EJ Coordinators and other staff with significant involvement in EJ program functions and activities. They strongly believed that AAs and RAs need to have the ability and flexibility to allocate and devote additional FTEs where necessary to accomplish crucial EJ functions and activities within their organizations. Therefore, they believed a good level of discretion is needed to be left with the AA or RA. However, they recognized the influence and effectiveness of the EJ program would be enhanced if OECA and OEJ had greater input into decisions regarding the allocation of FTEs to Headquarters programs and Regional offices. In this regard, creating an oversight role within OECA and OEJ could be a beneficial and appropriate thing to do. Most DAAs and DRAs agreed that creating a National Program Manager (NPM) for EJ (see Section 5) at an AA level would further enhance the influence and effectiveness of the EJ program.

Level and Consistency of Follow-up on National EJ Program Obligations: Data collected for this study revealed inconsistencies and often extremely late completion and submittal of crucial EJ program documents. Most importantly is the lateness of submittal of EJ action plans and EJ progress reports. As of the writing of this report, several final action plans and progress reports had yet be formally submitted to OEJ.

Benefits of Investing Staff and Other Resources for EJ: DAAs and DRAs were asked to identify the benefits of investing staff and other resources for EJ. Below are responses provided by DAAs and DRAs:

- Places EPA in a much better position to fulfill its primary goal of protecting human health and the environment

- Creates a sense of pride and commitment among the staff

- Encourages and promotes people to apply EJ to their job functions, which is crucial to conducting their jobs in an equitable way

- Helps staff provide a better and more complete focus for their regular work

- Provides tools to assist staff in applying EJ requirements and activities (for example, GIS tools and population information)

- Ensures response to communities is more effective

- Helps discover how severe an EJ problem exists at certain sites

- Shows that someone cares about their issues; it matters to people that their government will listen

- Builds trust and relationships with communities, thereby reducing complaints and addressing more environmental problems

- Helps better ensure environmental protection across the board, which is a core purpose of the Agency

- Makes the Region more aware of who the people are that they are trying to serve

- Provides greater access to stakeholders

- Defines points of contact on EJ matters

- Provides centralized staff with EJ expertise

- Enables Agency to strategically target EJ activities

- Provides for improved accountability

- Ensures that public health and environmental protection is equitably delivered

- Allows others to see and understand how their organization is playing a more active role in applying EJ to their work without having to be asked

- Improves the way their organization highlights how their work applies to and supports EJ

- Helps deal with a real need at the ground level that has traditionally not been adequately addressed from a public health and environmental quality standpoint

- Helps address a crucial need in numerous program areas of engaging affected communities and getting them involved (for example, the recent lead in water initiative)

Numerous DAAs and DRAs believed that in conjunction with these benefits, significant successes and lessons learned had been achieved and needed to be disseminated to all Headquarters and Regional organizations. In this regard, DAAs and DRAs urged that available

OEJ staff and other resources be focused on increasing and improving collection of this information, packaging it in a manner suitable for senior manager and staff use, and disseminating it in a timely manner.

Section 3: Integrating EJ into Strategic and Operating Plans

This section explores the area of opportunities to integrate EJ into the strategic and operating processes and plans in EPA Headquarters programs and Regional offices. The following provides a summary of the observations of the DAAs and DRAs, as well as pertinent data collected and assessed for this management study.

Knowledge and Understanding of EJ Coordinator Functions, Responsibilities and Activities: Most DAAs and DRAs indicated a general understanding of the daily functions and responsibilities of the EJ Coordinators. However, they acknowledged little understanding of the specific day-to-day activities the EJ Coordinators get involved in. In some cases, meetings between DAAs/DRAs and their EJ Coordinators have not occurred for months. Most DAAs and DRAs noted that their schedules and responsibilities make it challenging for them to know everything the EJ Coordinators are doing on a daily basis. However, most believed that front office organizational placement makes it easier for necessary interaction and meetings to occur when a specific issue needs their attention. They also acknowledged a high expectation and level of confidence that the EJ Coordinator would promptly bring to senior management attention EJ issues that crucially impact the Agency's ability to accomplish its mission. This is because EJ Coordinators are chosen for their sensitivity to EJ concerns; knowledge of and experience with EPA statutes, regulations and programs; and communications and outreach skills.

Alignment and Integration of EJ Action Plans and Strategic Plans and Operating Plans: Most DAAs and DRAs noted varying degrees of progress or effort toward integrating EJ action plans (and associated measures) into their strategic plans and operating plans. The relatively new nature of EJ action planning and measures of performance development seems to be an important and driving factor in the incomplete progress to date. Regardless of the progress, wide recognition exists that further progress needs to occur and that the commitment to do so exists and would be communicated to senior management and staff. Some DAAs and DRAs further stated the need for a more defined and systematic approach to accomplish better alignment and integration of EJ policies, programs and activities into overall strategic and operating plan processes. Several DAAs and DRAs suggested that additional guidance and support be provided by OEJ, including more refined and clear cut measures of performance and additional ideas and input on how to actually accomplish such alignment and integration.

Reporting of Important EJ Work Achievements and Accomplishments from Action, Strategic and Operating Plan Implementation: DAAs and DRAs universally indicated that excellent EJ work had been conducted and significant results had been achieved benefiting EJ communities. However, they also indicated a major impasse in getting these achievements and accomplishments effectively communicated across all Headquarters and Regional organizations. Various DAAs and DRAs noted that some information about their work had been provided to OEJ. It was agreed that OEJ, other Headquarters organizations, and the Regional offices need to work together in packaging and disseminating such information across all of EPA. Some DAAs and DRAs also noted this information needed to be in a user-friendly format, especially targeted for senior management and staff. Other DAAs and DRAs expressed movement toward the use of other methods to announce and celebrate EJ work achievements and accomplishments, which were either currently in use or being formulated. Two examples provided were use of awards programs and scheduling of various types of awareness activities. The topic needs to be discussed further by the EPA EJ Executive Steering Committee.

Coherent and Mutually Accepted National EJ Priorities: DAA and DRA discussions brought attention to their concerns about lack of a clear set of priorities for the EJ program. Various viewpoints were given for how this issue could be addressed. The most prominent suggestions DAAs and DRAs provided were:

- Convene a facilitated dialogue with the EJ Executive Steering Committee to reach a consensus on a set of national EJ priorities for FY05 and beyond

- Ensure that these national priorities, once established, are adequately and completely incorporated into EJ action plans and EPA strategic and operating plans

- Ensure that resources are aligned and available to fulfill EJ action plan and EPA strategic and operating plan requirements and activities

- Have OEJ review their own current priorities and consider realigning them with the realities of these national priorities

Senior Management Sensitivity to how EJ Issues Related to Their Program Management Responsibilities: Discussions during the April 2004 NEJAC meeting and various input from EJ Coordinators revealed that additional movement is necessary to further heighten Headquarters and Regional senior management sensitivities so they have a stronger link to their overall management responsibilities. These discussions indicated that by establishing some necessary drivers discussed in this report (e.g., creating an NPM for EJ, establishing a set of national priorities, and making Fundamentals of EJ training a priority not only for staff but for senior management), increased sensitivity would occur.

Section 4: Funding and Staffing for EJ

This section explores the area of Headquarters program and Regional office funding and staffing for EJ activities to ensure that adequate resources are available to fully implement the Agency's EJ programs. The following provides a summary of the observations of the DAAs and DRAs, as well as pertinent data collected and assessed for this management study.

Knowledge and Adequacy of FTEs Devoted to EJ Functions (People): Data collected for the management study, along with discussions with DAAs and DRAs, shows wide variations between Headquarters programs and Regional offices on the total number of FTEs devoted to EJ, including the EJ Coordinator and EJ support staff. During DAA and DRA discussions, there was little indication that a complete accounting of these FTE was well understood and readily available. Numerous DAAs and DRAs expressed varied levels of knowledge and understanding on the specific FTE levels reflected in their Headquarters program and Regional office EJ Action Plans. Many noted that they were confident this level of detail was understood and/or monitored by the EJ Coordinator. There was general consensus that the resources devoted to EJ are adequate to fulfill the commitments made in those plans and to ensure continued integration of EJ into their programs. However, this seemed to be a feeling they had without providing much in concrete to support this contention. Numerous DAAs and DRAs also volunteered without asking that the staffing decisions made – that is, the particular persons they assigned as EJ Coordinators – were good decisions from a personnel and skills mix perspective. Some DRAs also confirmed their need for additional resources in order to more completely fulfill their EJ requirements and activities at the Regional level. Two particular areas identified were additional travel funds to visit and interact with communities and additional grant dollars to support collaborative problem solving efforts and other community outreach initiatives.

Allocation of Dollar Resources (Contracts and Grants): Most DAAs and DRAs would support OEJ in obtaining additional resources that could be allocated to Headquarters program and Regional offices, especially additional grant and contract dollars. Numerous DAAs and DRAs also expressed a desire to have additional OEJ resources devoted to providing improved and value-added tools to support implementation of their EJ programs. Some examples provided were information on lessons learned and best practices, and user-friendly toolbox materials targeted more for senior staff and senior management. There were, however, varied views about what level of control OEJ should be provided generally for the allocation of dollar resources for EJ. Similar to FTE designation and allocation (see Section 2), numerous DAAs and DRAs felt it very important that AAs and RAs have the ability and flexibility to allocate and devote additional dollar resources where necessary to accomplish crucial EJ functions and activities within their organizations. It was agreed OEJ already has provided a major resource to Headquarters programs and Regional offices, the EJ Toolkit, which is a comprehensive EJ resource tool. A handy desk reference for the EJ Toolkit also is being made available. OEJ also has provided the EJ Geographic Assessment Tool to help EPA staff conduct EJ assessments. OEJ should solicit feedback on these and other tools that EPA staff may suggest to further assist their EJ responsibilities and activities.

Provision of Training on the Fundamentals of EJ: Discussions with DAAs and DRAs indicated their keen understanding of the importance of and high level of commitment to fulfilling Fundamentals of EJ training requirements for all employees. However, discussions also indicated a wide inconsistency in Headquarters program and Regional office urgency to undertake and administer Fundamental of EJ training to all organization staff and management. Some DAAs and DRAs provided estimates or targets for number of people trained per year that would require, in some cases, a couple to several years to cover all employees. Some DAAs and DRAs also indicated, however, that EJ Coordinators also have the difficult and challenging task of obtaining a good grounding in the various environmental statutes, policies and programs and that for the most part this is "on the job" training.

Development of Performance Expectations for EJ Coordinators and Other Significant EJ Staff: Nearly all DAAs and DRAs acknowledged a need to develop a core set of performance expectations for EJ Coordinators and other staff significantly involved in EJ functions and activities. Various DAAs and DRAs pointed out the unevenness in terms of adequacy of the performance standards and performance agreements of their EJ Coordinators. Many DAAs and DRAs also stated they would look upon OEJ to help Headquarters programs and Regional offices develop a set of minimum performance expectations and ensure they are consistently applied. Numerous DAAs and DRAs also wanted assurances that these performance standards could be revised, as well as augmented with additional measures, as necessary. The EPA EJ Executive Steering Committee should discuss this topic further.

Evaluation of Performance of EJ Coordinators and Other Significant EJ Staff: DAAs and DRAs identified various approaches that either are or could be used in gathering information and feedback on the performance of EJ Coordinators and other staff with significant EJ responsibilities (such as NEJAC Designated Federal Officials and EJ Steering Committee members). Approaches mentioned included the reactions of communities regarding EJ activities and initiatives undertaken for them, input from senior management and senior staff regarding their interaction, feedback from members of steering committees and NEJAC subcommittees, and feedback from OEJ. When asked about establishing a more routine approach for receiving OEJ input on the performance of EJ Coordinators and other staff with significant involvement in EJ programs and activities, DAAs and DRAs were favorable to and would encourage and accept such input. However, there was a good level of variation regarding whether the input should be formal or informal (e.g., a telephone conversation between the Director, OEJ and the appropriate DAA or DRA) in nature. Most DAAs and DRAs did not favor a formal OEJ role in assessing performance, and no DAA or DRA supported the Regional Counsel model with respect to EJ Coordinators reporting directly to OEJ. OEJ's preference would be to provide formal input on the performance of the EJ Coordinators.

Interaction Between EJ Coordinator and OEJ: Several DAAs and DRAs expressed a desire to see much more engagement of EJ Coordinators in communications and interactions with OEJ. Some DAAs and DRAs indicated that too much OEJ emphasis was placed on direct access and communication with AA/DAAs or RA/DRAs for issues and actions that could be first dealt with by the EJ Coordinators. These DAAs and DRAs further felt that EJ Coordinators could then appropriately determine the timing and manner to report to and/or seek involvement of senior management. Discussions with DAAs and DRAs provided a sense that they wanted their focus to be on policy and executive level issues, and that EJ Coordinators can and should focus on the details and bring more focused actions to AA/DAAs or RA/DRAs at the appropriate time for discussion and approval. However, OEJ has expressed concerns about the lack of adequate EJ Coordinator participation in the monthly EJ Coordinator conference calls, and, in some cases, complete absence from these conference calls.

EJ Coordinator Formal Interaction with and Reporting to AA/DAA or RA/DRA:
Discussions with DAAs and DRAs revealed that no consistent regimen of meetings and/or communications existed across all Headquarters and Regional organizations. While discussions indicated tacit approval and commitment for more frequent and formal communication (face-to-face program reviews and/or paper reports), no uniform and consistent movement towards this type of interaction seemed to be formally in the works across all Headquarters and Regional organizations.

Ways OEJ Could Better Assist Headquarters Programs and Regional Offices: DAAs and DRAs were asked to identify ways OEJ could better assist their organizations. Below are their responses:

- Face-to-face meetings, including periodic program reviews, to review status of activities and initiatives and share lessons learned

- Increased interaction with and reliance on EJ Coordinators rather than on senior managers

- Improved and more user-friendly tools to support EJ program implementation

- Consider "outside the box" activities and thinking that would further strengthen the national EJ program and improve coordination and communication with Headquarters and Regional organizations, including:

  o Week-long Regional reviews

  o Short-term details or "trades" of staff

- Examine additional mechanisms for providing more EJ resources support; especially helpful would be championing the funding of additional grant and cooperative agreement dollars and other resources

- Develop measures of success for a national EJ program, including possibly redefining the key priorities of OEJ

- Create more of a customer/supplier relationship with Headquarters and Regional organizations

- Improve role as an advocate, perhaps through periodic reports to or face-to-face meetings with AAs and RAs to highlight activities, successes and continuing challenges

- Solicit information on lessons learned and best practices and communicate them across all of EPA; possibly have these further formulated into national policy and guidelines

- Take the top five best practices and make them into national EJ policy and guidance, thereby increasing the pace of EJ integration across all of EPA

- Engage the EJ Executive Steering Committee to have a facilitated dialogue and reach consensus on a set of national EJ priorities

- Examine what the Regions are doing to add value with regard to EJ and communicate across all of EPA

- Create more user-friendly and less process-oriented policy direction, guidance documents and tools; for example, reconstitute the EJ toolkit into a real tool for senior management and senior staff to use in the field (usability and usefulness)

- Communicate which resources they can provide to help Regions address EJ

- Improve coordination with Headquarters and Regional organizations on guidance and policy

- Ensure continued funding of collaborative problem solving grants and other EJ grant programs

- Provide resources to support Geographic Information Systems (GIS), Land View, and other EJ tools, including training support on the use of these tools

Section 5: Shifting Resources and Formal Reporting Structures

This section explores the area of shifting resources and formal reporting structures to improve the integration of EJ into core programs in the Headquarters programs and Regional offices. The following provides a summary of the observations of the DAAs and DRAs, as well as pertinent data collected and assessed for this management study.

Relationship of EJ Coordinators and Their Organization's Senior Management:
Discussions with DAAs and DRAs revealed significant variation in the organizational placement of Headquarters program and Regional office EJ Coordinators. While most reside within a staff office within an AA's or RA's front office, the types of organization they are placed (i.e., functional responsibilities of those staff offices) differ from organization to organization. In very few instances does the EJ Coordinator have a direct reporting relationship with an AA/DAA or RA/DRA. In some cases, Regional location mirrors where OEJ is located within Headquarters; that is, within a Region's enforcement office. The major impact emphasized by these discussions is that EJ Coordinators typically have one layer of management to coordinate and communicate with before gaining access to the AA/DAA or RA/DRA. On the one hand, numerous DAAs and DRAs pointed out that placement of EJ Coordinators in a staff office of their front office provided them with ready access to tools and materials, as well as staff augmentation, which would not necessarily be the case if they reported directly to the AA/DAA or RA/DRA. On the other hand, given the crucial function of the EJ Coordinator, some DAAs and DRAs also stressed that they had an "open door policy" and urged their EJ Coordinators to make them aware and involved when an action or issue surfaces that needs their attention. For some DAAs and DRAs, having the EJ Coordinator placed in a staff office of their front office is necessary to balance the need to show the importance of EJ at the most senior level and keep everyone focused and attuned to EJ considerations in their work, with the realities of the institutional limitations of the AA/DAA's and RA/DRA's time.

Additional Organizational or Functional Realignment of EJ Coordinators Within Headquarters Programs and Regional Offices: Nearly every DAA and DRA indicated that little to no additional organizational or functional realignments would occur. However, one Regional office indicated that their EJ organizational model was being evaluated, and once completed, could lead to some additional changes, and one Headquarters program indicated that enhancements were being made to further integrate EJ into their requirements and activities. Also, a few Headquarters programs and Regional offices were identifying individuals within various program offices as EJ leads or contacts who would coordinate and communicate with the EJ Coordinator.

Reporting by EJ Coordinators to AAs/DRAs or RAs/DRAs: The approach taken to routinely receive reports (status and special) from EJ Coordinators also varies widely within each Headquarters program and Regional office. For example, while various AAs/DAAs and RAs/DRAs may receive some type of written report weekly, monthly or quarterly, actual routine meetings are sporadic. Some DAAs and DRAs go for months without meeting with their EJ Coordinator. There is no consistent rule or requirement established across Headquarters programs and Regional offices.

Interaction Between EJ Coordinators and EJ Steering Committees: The interaction between EJ Coordinators and EJ Steering Committees established by Headquarters programs and Regional offices also varies widely. Some meet on a bi-weekly basis, while others meet on a monthly, quarterly or much less frequent basis. Again, there is no consistent rule or requirement established across Headquarters programs and Regional offices.

Creation of a National Program Manager for EJ: Most DAAs and DRAs would support the official recognition of a National Program Manager (NPM) for EJ. Some noted that some NPM-like functions already existed within OEJ. Most DAAs and DRAs expressed the view that a political appointee would need to take on the designation as the NPM, and many identified the AA for the Office of Enforcement and Compliance Assurance (OECA) as a likely and appropriate candidate. Several DAAs and DRAs noted that an NPM for EJ, coupled with a base of resources (FTEs and contract and grant dollars), would enhance the commitment of Regional offices to tap into additional resources given the incentive coming from the NPM's budget allocation. Some DAAs and DRAs also noted that better accounting of resources and what they are accomplishing locally and nationally also could occur. A final point made by several DAAs and DRAs was that creation of an NPM for EJ should not detract from or replace the leadership needed from the AAs and RAs to ultimately make EJ a success. However, as noted above (Section 4), no DAA or DRA supported having EJ Coordinators report directly to the NPM for EJ. The NPM for EJ would oversee the integration of EJ activities into EPA Strategic and Operating Plans, track EJ resource allocation, and establish national EJ program priorities.

Integration of EJ at the State Level: DRAs provided insights on what is occurring at the State level regarding creation of EJ programs. DRAs noted that various discussions have and continue to occur with States, but some admitted that relationships needed to be improved regarding their integration of EJ and they were trying to work it out with States. Obvious from discussions with DRAs was that more concerted efforts were necessary at both Headquarters and Regional levels to engage States in adopting parallel and consistent EJ programs. Only one Region indicated success in having their States establish counterpart EJ Coordinators (Region 3).

Section 6: Findings & Recommendations

This section describes the findings reached based on the one-on-one discussions with EPA DAAs and DRAs, in-depth review of EPA Headquarters program and Regional office FY 2004-2005 EJ Action Plans and FY 2003 EJ Progress Reports, follow-up data requests made to EPA Headquarters program and Regional office EJ Coordinators, discussions at the April 12–16, 2004 NEJAC meeting, and discussions at the April 29, 2004 meeting of the Environmental Justice Executive Steering Committee.

This section also provides recommendations EPA and OEJ should further discuss and consider in their effort to continually improve and advance EPA's successful implementation of EJ programs, activities and policies within its Headquarters programs and Regional offices.

6.1 Designating Qualified and Committed Full Time Employees (FTEs)

1. Accounting for EJ Program FTEs

Finding 1: EPA programs and Regional offices need to adopt a consistent approach to accounting for EJ program FTEs. Some offices only account for those "core" FTE, which are substantially committed, or committed full-time, to EJ program functions. Examples include EJ Coordinator responsibilities, management of EJ grants, and EJ training. Other offices also account for those FTEs, which conduct EJ-related activities as a portion of their normal program responsibilities, e.g., as is the practice in EPA Regions 1 and 9, and the Office of Solid Waste and Emergency Response (OSWER). Examples include certain Brownfields projects, Superfund community involvement initiatives, and community air toxics pilot projects. However, it should be recognized that the number of FTEs devoted to EJ in each Headquarters program or Regional office will vary based on the particular circumstances that exist in their organization, and should not necessarily be looked upon as inconsistent with other program or office FTE commitments.

Recommendation 1: EPA needs to capture two categories of EJ program FTE in the future, "core" EJ program FTE, and total EJ-related FTE. This will minimize the current confusion caused by accounting for EJ program FTEs in different ways among Headquarters and Regional offices, and protect against the over-reporting or under-reporting of dedicated EJ FTEs throughout the Agency.

2. National Program Manager for EJ

Finding 2: OEJ has done a great job, with a limited number of FTE, of helping integrate EJ into EPA programs, activities, and policies. However, the influence and effectiveness of the EPA

EJ program would be enhanced if OECA and OEJ had greater input into EJ resources management and allocation decisions.

Recommendation 2: EPA should designate the AA for OECA as the National Program Manager (NPM) for Environmental Justice. This step would increase the influence and effectiveness of OEJ. The AA, OECA, would champion EJ at Senior EPA budget and planning meetings. The NPM for EJ would oversee the integration of EJ activities into the EPA Operating Plan and Strategic Plan; track EJ resource allocation across all EPA Headquarters programs and Regional offices; and establish national EJ program priorities.

3. EJ Program Resource Support

Finding 3: Senior EPA officials believe that the resources provided to them by OEJ, e.g., the Collaborative Problem Solving (CPS) grants program and the Environmental Careers Organization (ECO) cooperative agreement program, have been very helpful. ECO interns are allocated to EPA and community organizations to provide assistance in addressing public health and environmental concerns. At present, support is being provided for many ECO Associates. The first 30 CPS grants will be awarded during FY04 to provide significant support to affected communities.

Recommendation 3: EPA/OEJ should continue to provide support to other EPA organizations and communities through programs such as the CPS Grants Program, EJ Small Grants Program, and the ECO Associates Program. Further, OEJ should work with EPA National Program Managers to examine other mechanisms for providing additional EJ resource support to EPA programs.

4. EJ Program Contribution to Risk Reduction

Finding 4: EPA senior managers believe that investing in EJ has substantial benefits for EPA, including the following:

- Builds trust and relationship with communities;

- Reduces EJ complaints;

- Results in more public health and environmental problems being addressed due to the early alerts;

- Creates important new environmental initiatives; and\

- Ensures that public health and environmental protection is equitably delivered.

However, EPA has not done a good job of documenting how the investment in EJ has contributed to significant public health and environmental protection, e.g., risk reduction.

Recommendation 4: OEJ needs to work with the other Headquarters organizations and the 10 Regions to better document and communicate examples of how EJ activities have resulted in significant risk reduction. While it is clear that examples exist, senior managers and EJ Coordinators need to collect and communicate these important results. All EPA organizations must give higher priority to those EJ activities, which have the greatest public health and environmental benefits. Furthermore, EPA needs to develop performance measures (outputs and outcomes) for these activities. EPA also needs to develop performance measures for each of the communities receiving CPS grants. One recommended approach to better document and communicate how the Agency's investment in EJ has contributed to public health and environmental protection is for OEJ to collect, synthesize and summarize, and publicize EPA's EJ success stories concerning risk reduction. The EPA EJ Executive Steering Committee should discuss this important topic further.

5. EJ Action Plans and Progress Reports Resource Support

Finding 5: All EPA Headquarters programs and Regional offices have developed or are preparing FY 2004-2005 EJ Action Plans and FY 2003 Progress Reports. Based on review of these Plans and Progress Reports, and EPA senior management interviews, it appears that most of these organizations have adequate resources (staffing and funding) available to implement the activities in these plans. One Regional office expressed that adequate resources were not available to implement all activities in their plan, which inhibits the Region from addressing some very serious environmental disparities. This judgment for most EPA organizations might change if new program priorities are agreed upon in the future.

Recommendation 5: The Agency needs to continue this commitment to properly document and provide adequate resources to implement the activities and achieve the performance measures contained in these Plans and Progress Reports. These Plans and Progress Reports are a critical blueprint for implementation of EJ across all EPA activities, programs, and policies. It could be beneficial if OECA, OEJ and the EJ Executive Steering Committee aid in identifying and championing at the national level EJ target areas related to the Agency's strategic objectives that need policy and resource and FTE attention. Helping to ensure FTE allocation for "core" responsibilities could further enhance the credibility of the Agency's EJ efforts.

6. Lack of Timely Action Plans and Progress Reports

Finding 6: All Headquarters and Regional offices have obligations to prepare EJ Action Plans and EJ Progress Reports, and provide other important EJ program submissions to OEJ.

However, the documents are not being submitted in a timely fashion. In fact, they are extremely late. For example, FY04/05 EJ Action Plans were due on 12/31/03. Except for the timely submission by the Office of Environmental Information (OEI), no other Headquarters program submitted their Plan by the due date. Further, only Regions 1, 5 and 8 met the deadline. Almost five months after the deadline, three HQ/Regional offices have yet to submit their EJ Action Plans. No HQ/Regional office met the 2/28/04 deadline for submission of EJ Progress Reports, with approximately 12 Reports still pending.

Recommendation 6: EPA DAAs/DRAs and EJ Coordinators need to give a much higher priority to deadlines for preparation of these EJ Action Plans and EJ Progress Reports. The deadlines need to be taken seriously if EPA is to effectively implement its EJ program and meet the needs of affected communities. The EJ Executive Steering Committee needs to reaffirm the priority of this effort, and commit to meeting document submission deadlines in the future.

6.2   Integrating EJ into Strategic and Operating Plans

7. Communicating EJ Program Models of Success

Finding 7: Numerous EPA organizations in Headquarters and the Regions have conducted excellent EJ work, which has benefited impacted communities across the United States. However, this important work has not always been effectively communicated across all EPA national programs and Regional offices. As a result, important information is not being made available to all potential users. OSWER has begun to do this for the waste programs in Headquarters and the Regions. (See the report entitled, <u>OSWER Environmental Justice Success Stories Report [FY1999-2001]</u>).

Recommendation 7: It is recommended that OEJ, and the national program offices, document those most successful and significant EJ practices and/or lessons learned, which have been achieved by various EPA organizations, and disseminate these on a national level to all of EPA. OEJ should issue national guidance on the "top 5" EJ models of success. An example of important recent OEJ guidance is the EJ Toolkit. EPA should celebrate the most significant successes, e.g., via an annual EJ awards program. OEJ, as the overall lead for the Agency's national EJ program, should continue to have primary responsibility for collecting, synthesizing and summarizing, and publicizing model achievements throughout the Agency, and particularly to DAAs, DRAs and EJ Coordinators. However, since many of these models of success should be captured in EJ Progress Reports, EPA senior managers need to place much higher priority on producing high quality and timely EJ Progress Reports.

8. Improving Program Coordination and Communication

Finding 8: While the mission of the Office of Environmental Justice has not changed since it was established in 1992, OEJ should take on new and/or different activities to further strengthen the national EJ program. Those activities relate to improving coordination and communication between OEJ and the Headquarters programs and Regional offices.

Recommendation 8: OEJ should designate someone to be a focal point for national EJ program coordination and integration. OEJ should also conduct annual EJ program reviews of half of the 10 Regional offices. A senior manager from OEJ should spend up to one week in each Regional office to review all aspects of EPA Regional EJ program activities, policies, and operational procedures. These additional activities, not limited to the two above, may necessitate an increase in resources for OEJ.

9. EPA Management Sensitivity to EJ Issues

Finding 9: Senior EPA managers in Headquarters and the Regions need to obtain a greater sensitivity regarding how EJ issues relate to their program management responsibilities. This is critical to help ensure that senior managers and their staff understand how EJ relates to regulations development, permitting, cleanup, enforcement, and numerous other EPA responsibilities.

Recommendation 9: There needs to be a reaffirmation of EJ as a priority by the EPA Administrator. Each Headquarters media program manager and RA/DRA needs to have a substantive meeting at least once annually with a least one EJ organization impacted by the programs they administer. Each senior manager needs to take EJ Fundamentals Training, and make sure that staff does likewise. EJ needs to be a topic on the agenda when senior managers convene important internal meetings, meetings with States and other partners, and meetings with key stakeholders. EPA management needs to demonstrate a real commitment and sensitivity to EJ issues.

10. Need for National EJ Program Priorities

Finding 10: OEJ, other Headquarters programs, and the Regional offices have all conducted important EJ activities for more than a decade to implement EPA's EJ mission. However, there is not mutual agreement on national EJ priorities for the future.

Recommendation 10: Under the leadership of OEJ, the EJ Executive Steering Committee should convene to have a facilitated dialogue and reach consensus agreement on a set of national EJ priorities and associated performance measures that are designed to integrate EJ across all EPA programs for FY2005 and beyond. These resulting priorities, and associated resource needs, should be integrated into updates to the EJ Action Plans, EPA Operating Plan, and EPA Strategic Plan.

11. Integration of EJ Activities into Strategic and Operating Plans

Finding 11: EJ Action Plans have been prepared for FY03, and FY04/05. These Plans serve as the blueprint for EJ performance across EPA Headquarters programs and Regional offices. However, these Plans need to be better aligned with EPA Operating Plan and Strategic Plan processes. Some steps in this direction are being taken, however, much more needs to be done. All EPA Regional offices are required to prepare Regional Strategic Plans. These Plans are now being completed. These Plans are an ideal place to document further commitments to environmental justice. The national EPA Operating Plan and the Strategic Plan have EJ components. Several Regions have incorporated EJ activities into their operating plans.

Recommendation 11: All Headquarters programs and Regional offices should incorporate all significant EJ activities into their respective Strategic Plans and operating plans. EPA national program managers need to fully integrate EJ activities into the Agency's FY2005 Operating Plan and next update to the EPA Strategic Plan. The NPM for EJ should be tasked to work with other NPMs to ensure the full integration of EJ activities and performance measures into the Agency Operating Plan and the Strategic Plan. The facilitated dialogue by the EPA EJ Executive Steering Committee should provide important input to this process.

6.3 Funding and Staffing for EJ

12. Need for More EJ Training for EPA Managers and Staff

Finding 12: The Fundamentals of EJ training is critical to the EPA's goal to integrate EJ into all EPA programs, activities, and policies. Some EPA Regions, e.g., EPA Regions 1 and 9, have been very aggressive at training their staff on EJ fundamentals and principles. However, some EPA Regions and most EPA Headquarters national programs have a sizable portion of their staff that has not received EJ training to date. Others conducted EJ training in their organization more than 5 years ago. This training is critical to achieving an "EJ mindset" within all EJ managers and staff, and integrating EJ into all EPA activities, programs, and policies.

Recommendation 12: EPA should make it mandatory that all managers and appropriate staff take EJ training over the next three years. EPA managers, particularly in Headquarters, need to make such training a much higher priority. EPA Headquarters programs and Regional offices need to develop an in-house capability to train their managers and staff. EPA DRAs and DAAs should provide OEJ by 9/1/04 with a schedule and plan for achieving this goal in each Regional/Headquarters organization.

13. Role of EJ Coordinators

Finding 13: There is some inconsistency in terms of how EJ Coordinators support Headquarters and Regional management, as well as how they interact with Headquarters and Regional programs. EPA should take some actions to improve this state of affairs, i.e., achieve greater consistency in the role of EJ Coordinators.

Recommendation 13: EPA should improve the EJ Coordinator function by doing the following:

- OEJ, HQ programs, and Regional offices should develop a set of minimum performance expectations for all EJ Coordinators, e.g., EJ Coordinators all need to take the Fundamentals of EJ training; should meet at least monthly with other members of their organization's EJ team; and should coordinate EJ training throughout their organizations.

- OEJ should provide input annually, as part of the performance evaluation cycle, to HQ and Regional offices, on the performance of EJ Coordinators.

- OEJ should work with EJ Coordinators to establish a timely and effective reporting process. For example, brief, 2-page progress reports each quarter on EJ Coordinator activities for the previous quarter could be prepared and obtained.

- DAAs/DRAs should commit to frequent meetings with EJ Coordinators, i.e., at least once a month.

- OEJ and the EJ Executive Steering Committee need to made the EJ Coordinators a more integral component of the national EJ program. These EJ Coordinators need more direct interactions with OEJ management and should attend joint meetings with the EPA EJ Executive Steering Committee on a periodic basis.

6.4 Shifting Resources and Formal Reporting Structures

14. Relation of DAAs/DRAs to EJ Coordinators

Finding 14: The EJ Executive Steering Committee, composed primarily of the OEJ Director, DAAs and DRAs, is an effective mechanism to bring senior management attention to EPA's environmental justice program. However, there is variation across the Headquarters programs and Regional offices regarding how the EJ Coordinators and the core, full-time EJ team, within the various EPA organizations relate to these senior officials. In some cases, the EJ Coordinator reports directly to a DAA or DRA; however, in most cases, the EJ Coordinator reports to an Office Director or Division Director in charge of a cross-cutting organization, who then reports to a DAA or DRA. It is important that there be frequent interaction between the Executive Steering Committee member and the EJ Coordinator.

Recommendation 14: It is recommended and clearly preferable that the EJ Coordinator report directly to the DAA or DRA. At a minimum, it is recommended that each Headquarters program and Regional Office put in place mechanisms to ensure that the DAA, DRA and/or Executive Steering Committee member and the EJ Coordinator meet at least once a month to discuss important EJ issues and the status of implementation of the FY04/05 EJ Action Plan. The entire EJ team in an organization should meet with the DAA or DRA at least quarterly.

15. Creation of State EJ Programs

Finding 15: Due to the delegation of many EPA programs to the States, it is critical that the EPA Regions work with their State partners to create a strong EJ program presence within the States. This is the only way to ensure effective integration of EJ into all environmental programs, activities, and policies. For example, EPA Region 3 has been successful in getting its 5 States and the District of Columbia to establish an EJ Coordinator in each of these organizations.

Recommendation 15: It is recommended that each EPA Headquarters program and Regional office work with the States, Environmental Commissioners of the States (ECOS), and other organizations to create an EJ function within each of the States, territories, and other governmental jurisdictions which EPA relies on to implement environmental statutes and associated regulations. This activity and associated performance measures should be incorporated into the next update of the EJ Action Plans.

List of Appendices

Appendix 1: Areas of Inquiry for EPA Deputy Assistant Administrator (DAA) and Deputy Regional Administrator (DRA) Discussions

Appendix 2: List and Schedule of EPA Deputy Assistant Administrator (DAA) and Deputy Regional Administrator (DRA) Discussions

Appendix 3: Template for Summary of EPA Deputy Assistant Administrator (DAA) and Deputy Regional Administrator (DRA) Discussions

Appendix 4: List of EPA Headquarters Program and Regional Office FY 2004-2005 EJ Action Plans and FY 2003 EJ Progress Reports Reviewed for the Management Study

Appendix 5: List of Follow-up Data Requested from EPA Headquarters Program and Regional Office EJ Coordinators

Appendix 6: Various Tables and Charts Summarizing Data and Other Information Gathered and Reviewed As Part of the Management Study

Appendix 1
U.S. Environmental Protection Agency (EPA)
Environmental Justice (EJ) Program Comprehensive Management Study

Areas of Inquiry for EPA Deputy Regional Administrator (DRA) and
Deputy Assistant Administrator (DAA) Discussions

I. Designating Qualified and Committed Full-Time Employees (FTEs)

1. What resources were dedicated to EJ program support in FY03? What are the resources dedicated for FY04? Please express your answer in terms of full-time equivalent (FTE) staff, contract dollars, grant dollars, and other applicable resources. How are these resources allocated in your organization?
2. How are the EJ program staff positions in your organization funded? For example, do you use discretionary funds and/or program funds?
3. How are EJ activities funded?
4. What are the similarities and/or differences in the way you staff and fund your organization's EJ requirements and activities, as compared to other Headquarters and Regional organizations you are familiar with? For example, point out any funding inconsistencies and/or staffing disparities.
5. Are resources allocated (FTE/$) for each activity listed in your FY04-05 EJ Action Plan? Are these resources adequate? If not, what areas would you invest additional staff and/or dollars?
6. Is your organization's current funding and staffing levels adequate to fulfill the commitments in your FY04-05 EJ Action Plan? If not, what adjustments are necessary? Please express in terms of necessary increases or realignments of staff and/or funding resources.
7. What benefits does EPA gain in assigning staff and funding resources to support and implement EJ requirements and activities? Please express in terms of tangible and intangible benefits.
8. Are there any particular organizational elements within your organization that would beneficially improve their integration of EJ if EJ resources were redirected to them? If not, why not?
9. Are your organization's resources adequate to provide effective monitoring, evaluation and reporting of the activities in your organization's FY04-05 EJ Action Plan? Are they adequate to also undertake corrections in program deficiencies as identified?
10. How are EJ activities reflected in your overall operating budget?

II. Integrating EJ into Strategic and Operating Plans

1. Do you maintain direct and regular contact with your EJ coordinator (and other staff with related EJ responsibilities) on specific issues regarding the implementation of your EJ Action Plan?
2. Do you meet regularly with your EJ staff to track and measure the progress in the implementation of the EJ Action Plan?

3. What improvements or actions have been taken to better integrate EJ activities, programs, and policies into your organization's strategic plan and operating plan processes? Do you foresee future additional opportunities and/or actions that will further facilitate this integration? If yes, please outline those specific opportunities and/or actions.
4. How are you measuring your success in the FY04-05 EJ Action Plan, in terms of outputs and outcomes?
5. Which FY04-05 EJ Action Plan activities should be designated as GPRA elements? Which of your organization's EJ-related activities have a "J" budget code?
6. How are EJ activities, programs, and policies coordinated within your organization? How does coordination occur between your organization and other Headquarters and Regional organizations?
7. Have you reviewed OEJ's suggestions on <u>Developing an Effective Environmental Justice Program</u> (issued in 2002)? If yes, did you consider and/or use the suggestions when designing your organization's current EJ program?
8. What changes in staffing, funding, and/or organization are necessary to make EJ a greater EPA priority?
9. What should EPA do in the future to better align the agency's EJ Action Plans, EPA Strategic Plan, and Agency Operating Plan?
10. Which are the best options for increasing the influence or authority of OEJ over EPA's Headquarters and Regional EJ programs? What would be the implications of various alternatives on OEJ?
    a. Should EJ Coordinators report to OEJ? Would this result in greater consistency in EJ program decision-making?
    b. Are there other options for achieving the goal of greater consistency in EJ program implementation? For example, should OEJ and your organization co-manage the EJ Coordinators?

III. Funding and Staffing for EJ

1. How many staff is assigned to work on EJ functions in your organization? What is the organizational location of these staff? How many staff is assigned to EJ functions on a full-time basis? How many staff work on EJ activities as a collateral duty?
2. Are you aware of your EJ coordinator's daily functions and responsibilities?
3. Are the responsibilities of your formally assigned EJ personnel adequate enough to integrate EJ into your programs?
4. What is the skill mix of the EJ staff within your organization? Is this skill mix adequate to meet the needs and demands of your specific EJ requirements and activities? If not, what changes would you make and how would you go about making those changes?
5. Does your staff have a thorough understanding of all your programs and have contacts across your offices in order to mobilize support and cooperation, and provide assistance in integrating EJ into the decision-making process?
6. Does your staff possess a thorough understanding of environmental justice in relation to existing environmental laws (not civil rights laws)? Has your staff completed the basic Fundamentals of EJ course?
7. How is the use of existing statutory authorities manifested in your FY04-05 EJ Action Plan?

8. Are EJ responsibilities adequately incorporated into the position descriptions of the EJ Coordinator and other staff positions with significant EJ program responsibility in your organization? Regardless of their adequacy, does each employee have established performance agreements related to their EJ responsibilities? (Please provide a copy of appropriate staff position descriptions and performance agreements.)

9. How is the success of your EJ program reflected in your staff's performance evaluation?

10. What are your views on having the EJ Coordinator in your organization reporting to EPA's Office of Environmental Justice (OEJ) to better integrate EJ into EPA programs? (Please express your views in terms of advantages and disadvantages.)

IV. **Staffing Resources and Formal Reporting Structures**

1. When was the EJ function in your organization originally created (fiscal year)?

2. Where is the organizational placement of the EJ function in your organization? (Please provide a copy of an applicable organizational chart or organizational list.) Why was it placed there? Why should it remain there from the point of view of integrating EJ into the decision-making process?

3. How is your office organized to carry out environmental justice activities across your programs?

4. Have any organizational changes occurred since the initial inception of the EJ function in your organization? If yes, when did these changes occur and for what reasons? If no, are there any organizational changes anticipated or planned in the future?

5. Regardless of whether organizational changes have occurred or are planned to occur, what changes would you recommend to your organization's EJ program? Examples could include enhancements to or realignment of staffing and funding and changes to the infrastructure of the EJ organizational approach within your entire organization? For those you do identify, how would you go about making the changes?

Appendix 2

List and Schedule of EPA Deputy Assistant Administrator and

Deputy Regional Administrator Discussions

EPA Office	Date	Time	EPA DAA/DRA	E-mail Address	Call Number
Region 1	Tu 4/6/04	8:30-10:00am	Ira Leighton	leighton.ira@epa.gov	617-918-1011
Region 2	Tu 4/20/04	9:00-10:30am	Kathy Callahan	callahan.kathy@epa.gov	212-637-5000
Region 3	Fr 4/2/04	3:00-4:30pm	Tom Voltaggio	voltaggio.tom@epa.gov	215-814-3125
Region 4	Th 4/1/04	2:00-3:30pm	Stan Meiburg	meiburg.stan@epa.gov	404-562-8357
Region 5	Fr 4/9/04	11:00-12:30pm	Bharat Mathur	mathur.bharat@epa.gov	312-886-3000
Region 6	Tu 4/6/04	11:00-12:30pm	Larry Starfield	starfield.lawrence@epa.gov	214-665-2100
Region 7	Mo 4/12/04	1:00-2:30pm	Bill Rice	rice.william@epa.gov	913-551-7823
Region 8	Th 4/8/04	5:30-7:00pm	Carol Rushin	rushin.carol@epa.gov	303-312-6976
Region 9	We 4/7/04	5:00-6:30pm	Laura Yoshii	yoshii.laura@epa.gov	415-947-8702
Region 10	Tu 4/6/20	5:00-6:30pm	Ron Kreizenbeck	kreizenbeck.ron@epa.gov	206-553-1265
OSWER	Tu 4/20/04	11:00-12:30pm	Barry Breen	breen.barry@epa.gov	202-566-0200
OECA	Th 4/15/04	7:30-9:00am	Phyllis Harris	harris.phyllis@epa.gov	202-564-2440
OECA	Th 3/25/04	3:00-4:30pm	Mike Walker	walker.mike@epa.gov	202-564-2626
OPPTS	Fr 4/23/04	9:00-10:00	Margaret Schneider	schneider.margaret@epa.gov	202-564-0554
OAR	We 4/21/04	3:00-4:30pm	Rob Brenner	brenner.rob@epa.gov	202-564-1677
OW	Fr 4/9/04	3:30-5:00pm	Mike Shapiro	shapiro.mike@epa.gov	202-564-5700
ORD	We 4/7/04	9:00-10:30am	William (Bill) Farland	farland.william@epa.gov	202-564-6620
OIA	Fr 4/9/04	9:00-10:30 am	Jerry Clifford	clifford.jerry@epa.gov	202-564-6600
OEI	Fr 4/23/04	10:30-12:00pm	Linda Travers	travers.linda@epa.gov	202-564-6665
OPEI	Th 4/22/04	4:00-5:30pm	Louise Wise	wise.louise@epa.gov	202-564-4332
OCFO	Fr 4/23/04	2:00-3:00pm	Mike Ryan	ryan.mike@epa.gov	202-564-1152

U.S. Environmental Protection Agency (EPA)
Environmental Justice (EJ) Program Comprehensive Management Study

Template for Summary of EPA Deputy Assistant Administrator (DAA) and
Deputy Regional Administrator (DRA) Discussions

Discussion Data

EPA DAA/DRA Name and Title:
Headquarters Program/Regional Office:
Date and Time of Discussion:
Discussion Lead and Support:

Discussion Executive Summary

I.   Designating Qualified and Committed Full Time Employees (FTEs)

Reserved.

II.   Integrating EJ Into Strategic and Operating Plans

Reserved.

III.   Funding and Staffing for EJ

Reserved.

IV.   Staffing Resources and Formal Reporting Structures

Reserved.

Appendix 4
U.S. Environmental Protection Agency (EPA)
Environmental Justice (EJ) Program Comprehensive Management Study

**List of EPA Headquarters Program and Regional Office FY 2004-2005 EJ Action Plans
and FY 2003 EJ Progress Reports Reviewed for the Management Study**

EPA Headquarters Programs and Regional Offices	FY 2004-2005 EJ Action Plan	FY 2003 EJ Progress Report
Office of Air and Radiation (OAR)	✔	✔
Office of Enforcement and Compliance Assurance (OECA)		
Office of Environmental Information (OEI)	✔	✔
Office of International Affairs (OIA)	✔	
Office of Policy, Economics, and Innovation (OPEI)	✔	
Office of Prevention, Pesticides and Toxic Substances (OPPTS)	✔	
Office of Research and Development (ORD)		
Office of Solid Waste and Emergency Response (OSWER)	✔	✔
Office of Water (OW)	✔	
Region 1	✔	✔
Region 2	✔	
Region 3	✔	
Region 4	✔	
Region 5	✔	
Region 6	✔	✔
Region 7	✔	✔
Region 8	✔	✔
Region 9	✔	
Region 10		

Appendix 5
U.S. Environmental Protection Agency (EPA)
Environmental Justice (EJ) Program Comprehensive Management Study

List of Follow-up Data Requested from EPA Headquarters Program and
Regional Office EJ Coordinators

- When was the EJ function in your organization originally created (fiscal year)?

- Where is the organizational placement of the EJ function in your organization? (Please provide a copy of an applicable organizational chart or organizational list.) Why was it placed there? Why should it remain there from the point of view of integrating EJ into the decision-making process?

- How many staff are assigned to work on EJ functions in your organization? What is the organizational location of these staff? How many staff are assigned to EJ functions on a full-time basis? How many staff work on EJ activities as a collateral duty?

- Are EJ responsibilities adequately incorporated into the position descriptions of the EJ Coordinator and other staff positions with significant EJ program responsibility in your organization? Regardless of their adequacy, does each employee have established performance agreements related to their EJ responsibilities? (Please provide a copy of appropriate staff position descriptions and performance agreements.)

- What resources were dedicated to EJ program support in FY03? What are the resources dedicated for FY04? Please express your answer in terms of full-time equivalent (FTE) staff, contract dollars, grant dollars, and other applicable resources. How are these resources allocated in your organization?

- Which FY04-05 EJ Action Plan activities should be designated as GPRA elements? Which of your organization's EJ-related activities have a "J" budget code?

- How are EJ activities, programs, and policies coordinated within your organization? How does coordination occur between your organization and other Headquarters and Regional organizations?

Appendix 6-A
U.S. Environmental Protection Agency (EPA)
Environmental Justice (EJ) Program Comprehensive Management Study

Reported EPA Headquarters Program and Regional Offices Environmental Justice Full Time Equivalent Staff – Core and Collateral

EPA Headquarters Programs and Regional Offices	Number of FTE	
	Core	Core/Collateral
Office of Air and Radiation (OAR)	2	6
Office of Enforcement and Compliance Assurance (OECA)	1	16
Office of Environmental Information (OEI)	0	2.5
Office of International Affairs (OIA)	0.5	4.7
Office of Policy, Economics, and Innovation (OPEI)	1	2
Office of Prevention, Pesticides and Toxic Substances (OPPTS)	3	18
Office of Research and Development (ORD)	0	2
Office of Solid Waste and Emergency Response (OSWER)	1	23.7
Office of Water (OW)	1	15
Region 1	3	14
Region 2	2	3
Region 3	3	3
Region 4	1	5.5
Region 5	2	3.5
Region 6	5	18
Region 7	4	6
Region 8	5.5	5.5
Region 9	5	51
Region 10	1	2
Totals	41	199.4

Appendix 6-B
U.S. Environmental Protection Agency (EPA)
Environmental Justice (EJ) Program Comprehensive Management Study

Reported EPA Headquarters Program and Regional Offices Environmental Justice Program Placement

EPA Headquarters Programs and Regional Offices	Program Placement	
	DAA's/DRA's Office	Cross-Cutting Division
Office of Air and Radiation (OAR)		✔
Office of Enforcement and Compliance Assurance (OECA)		✔
Office of Environmental Information (OEI)	✔	
Office of International Affairs (OIA)		✔
Office of Policy, Economics, and Innovation (OPEI)	✔	
Office of Prevention, Pesticides and Toxic Substances (OPPTS)	✔	
Office of Research and Development (ORD)		✔
Office of Solid Waste and Emergency Response (OSWER)	✔	
Office of Water (OW)	✔	
Region 1	✔	
Region 2	✔	
Region 3		✔
Region 4	✔	
Region 5		✔
Region 6	✔	
Region 7		✔
Region 8		✔
Region 9		✔
Region 10	✔	

Appendix 6-C
U.S. Environmental Protection Agency (EPA)
Environmental Justice (EJ) Program Comprehensive Management Study

Reported EPA Headquarters Program and Regional Offices
Environmental Justice Training Achieved/Planned

EPA Headquarters Programs and Regional Offices	Number of Staff Trained	
	To Date	Planned for FY04
Office of Air and Radiation (OAR)	100	120
Office of Enforcement and Compliance Assurance (OECA)	30	~200
Office of Environmental Information (OEI)	4	20
Office of International Affairs (OIA)	5	60
Office of Policy, Economics, and Innovation (OPEI)	~10	No estimate
Office of Prevention, Pesticides and Toxic Substances (OPPTS)	5	375 by end of FY06
Office of Research and Development (ORD)	6	1,900 by end of FY06
Office of Solid Waste and Emergency Response (OSWER)	85	~100
Office of Water (OW)	15	30
Region 1	712	20
Region 2	650+	New staff trained as needed
Region 3	250+	New staff trained as needed
Region 4	350	125
Region 5	400	No estimate
Region 6	308	50
Region 7	15	30
Region 8	300	100
Region 9	~500	315
Region 10	28	110